PARENTING DIGITAL NATIVES

What parents can do about the dangers of social media

Dr. Lauretta Justin

Parenting Digital Natives: What parents can do about the dangers of social media

By Dr. Lauretta Justin

ISBN-13: 978-0-9971126-6-5

Book Categories: Family, Parenting, Relationships, Self Help, Motivational and Inspirational, Personal Growth, Success.

Keywords: Family, Relationships, Parenting, Children, Technology Usage, Teenagers, Personal growth

DrLaurettaJustin.com
6601 Old Winter Garden Rd. Suite 104
Orlando, FL 32835

Contents

Contents

Parenting Digital Natives

The widespread adoption of various digital technologies by today's teenagers has added a modern wrinkle to a universal challenge of parenthood– specifically, striking a balance between allowing independent exploration and providing an appropriate level of parental oversight. Social media is the new social currency for these digital natives. Digital connectivity offers many potential benefits from connecting with peers to accessing educational content. However, many parents are concerned about the behaviors teens engage in online, the people with whom they interact and the personal information they give out. Indeed, these concerns are not limited to parents. Lawmakers and advocates have raised concerns about issues such as online safety, cyber bullying and privacy issues affecting teens. Here are some of the reasons for these concerns:

- About 75% of teens have smart phones, 95% of them are online, and 70% spend more than 17 hours per week online.
- They don't email or talk on the phone, they text, facetime or Skype.
- Although they are immersed in the digital world, they often lack the basic skills to enhance technology use. For example, they take selfies at home without turning off the geo tracking on their phones.
- They don't perceive privacy as older generations do. Teens share a wide range of information about themselves on social media sites; indeed,

the sites themselves are designed to encourage the sharing of information and the expansion of networks.

According to Pew Research Center, here are some of the challenges that teens face on social media:

1. **Posting of personal information**
   - 92% post their **real name**
   - 91% post a **photo of themselves**
   - 84% post their **interests**, such as movies, music, or books they like
   - 82% post their **birth date**
   - 71% post their **school name**
   - 71% post the **city or town where they live**
   - 62% post their **relationship status**
   - 53% post their **email address**
   - 24% post **videos of themselves**
   - 20% post their **cell phone number**

2. **Unintentional Posting of illegal activities**
   a. Example, 2 South Portland, Maine teens posted a video on YouTube showing themselves placing a kitten in the microwave and appearing to turn it on. A 10 sec clip of the video shows up on Twitter. Someone from an animal protection agency saw the 10 sec video and got concerned. After the authorities were contacted, the teens were issued summons to appear on animal cruelty

charges. The truth is they never did put a cat in a microwave. But because it appeared as if they did in the video, they were charged.

3. **Making unintended threats**
   a. A teenage boy bullied on social media gets mad and makes threat to shoot up the school cafeteria. Even though he had no priors and was genuinely sorry for making this threat online, he was arrested and charged with criminal charges. He didn't mean to do it, he just "snapped".

4. **Cyberstalking**
   a. To communicate words, images… through electronic mail or communication directed at a specific person, causing substantial emotional distress to that person and serving no legitimate purpose. Florida Statute §784.048.
   b. Cyberstalking can lead to 1st degree misdemeanor and 1 year in Jail
   c. Aggravated Cyberstalking include a threat of someone under 16 and it equals a 3rd degree felony and up to 5 years in Jail.

5. **Online solicitation and Sexting**
   a. Sexual Predators use Social Media to contact victims. Their prime target age for victims are 11-15. 33% of teens are friends

with someone they don't know on social media, that puts them at risk.

b. Apps of concern for online solicitation – Favorites of sexual predators.

   i. **Kik Messenger** is a free app that lets you easily communicate with all your friends and contacts, sending them text messages, pictures, and chatting with them in real time. One of the features that makes Kik Messenger unique is its integrated web browser. This lets you open any hyperlink that you receive without leaving the app, which can save you lots of time. Kik Messenger – Apple store rating from 9+ to 12+ for "Mild sexual content and nudity." However most other rating organizations give it 17+. The companion apps that come with it present a bigger danger. Apps such as: Hit me up.

   ii. **Tumblr** rated 17+ in the App Store has more porn than most porn sites and it's free. According to Wikipedia Tumblr is a microblogging platform and social networking website founded by David Karp in 2007, and owned by Yahoo! since 2013. The service allows users to post

4

multimedia and other content to a short-form blog.

iii. Boys are groomed by predators using gaming sites with text and chat features such as **Minecraft, Clash Clans and Xbox live**

iv. **Twitter** has been used as a vehicle for recruitment of girls to amateur porn industry. The porn industry uses Twitter to recruit customers for their paid sites. Just google it!

v. **Whisper App** rated 17+ encourages users to tell secrets and say things they can't say other places. It's been linked to numerous sexual assaults. Often used by law enforcement in sting operations.

6. Cyberbullying

a. Apps of concern for cyberbullying: Intending to keep parents and school officials out.

i. **Ask.fm**, rated 12+ years old: Over 150Million users love ASKfm! ASKfm is the #1 Q&A app where you find out more about your friends by seeing their answers to questions you send their way. Ask anonymously or not. It's entertaining, easy to use, and you'll be surprised how much you learn about other people and even yourself. Every day around the world, ASKfm users are asking and answering over millions of questions in over 40 languages.

ii. **After School App**, rated 17+: Intended to keep parents and school officials out. Parents need to know that *After School* uses kids' Facebook profiles to verify they're students at a specific high school before granting access to the school's page within the app. From there, teens see images and posts created anonymously by other students or can create anonymous posts themselves. The app was removed from the app store after complaints from school administrators about bullying incidents and has since been updated with moderation and tighter age-verification. A live moderator reviews every post and tags each with the type of content it contains. Teens 13 and up can register, but to see posts tagged with "sex," "drugs," "profanity," or "gross," teens must verify they're over 17 by scanning the code on their ID cards.

7. **Creating an online persona that glamorizes drugs or violence**
    a. Example of a 15-year-old arrested for making threats because he posted song lyrics from Eminem's song "I'm back" without any association with the author. The authorities automatically assumed that the post was original. He was arrested and later acquitted, but nevertheless arrested.
    b. If the post is not original, always attach the name of the author.

Who are the Digital Natives?

Digital natives are individuals born or brought up during the digital technology era; and therefore are familiar with computers, portable devices, tablets, smart phones, the Internet and social media from an early age.

What you can do to protect your kids online and on social media

So, what can parents do about the dangers of social media?

1. Talk to your kids and instruct them on how to be responsible on Social Media.

2. Set family guidelines for your household. Require your children to follow your guidelines for the use of digital devices or take them away. They are children, they need to be protected. Be the parent and create your own firewall around your family.

3. Create a profile on many social media platforms yourself so you can learn to speak the language and know who your kids are communicating with. Get involved and invade their privacy; they are only children. There are online resources you can use to learn about the applications your kids are using. Here are a few:
   a. Commonsensemedia.org
   b. Wiredsafety.org
   c. Cybersafebook.com
   d. Family Online Safety Institute – fosi.org

4. Consider getting a monitoring software such as:
   a. **MobileSpy App** – Not Free
      i. Tracks GPS Location

11

ii. Monitor Web Browsing

iii. Call History Logs

iv. Browse Text Messages

v. View Instant Message (IM) Chats

vi. Scan Multimedia Files

b. **SociallyActive.com** – Not free

i. SociallyActive is like mission control for parents. **We bring your child's entire digital presence into clear view** for you and provide you with useful tools to help you need to help you help your teen navigate and steer clear of potential dangers online.

c. **NetNanny.com** – Not Free

i. Internet Filter: Be in control of your internet. Set filtering for 18 categories of online content to either block, warn, or allow for view.

ii. Block Pornography: Warn or block access to pornography and other adult content.

iii. Time Management: Set the total number of Internet hours in a day or set specific times of the day when your child can be online.

iv. Mask Profanity: View a web page without being bombarded by vulgar language.

v. Social Media Monitoring: Net Nanny Social helps protect kids from online threats and monitors activities related to your child's "friends," cyberbullying, sexual predators, privacy concerns, and reputation-damaging pictures or videos.

vi. Alerts and Reporting: Receive reports and mail alerts about your child's online activity.

vii. Remote Admin: Check usage reports, change your child's profile settings, and much more, from any computer with an Internet connection. [learn more]

viii. User Profiles: Use preset user profiles or customize settings for each family member; unlimited user profiles for each computer.

d. **Webwatcher.com** – FREE

    i. WebWatcher is the #1 rated Parental Monitoring Software, offering a full family of monitoring software compatible with iPhone, Android, PC and Mac. All WebWatcher products install easily in 5 minutes or less, are undetectable (thus tamper proof) and all recorded data is sent to a secure web-based account which allows you to monitor kids and employees at your convenience from any computer. WebWatcher allows you to monitor multiple devices (such as a PC and an iPhone) from the same user interface so you get one unified view (1 license needed for each device)

e. **Teensafe.org** – Not Free, Works with both Apple and Samsung phones. It links to a nightly backup and allows you to:

    i. Read texts

    ii. Recover deleted texts

    iii. See a phone call log

    iv. See web search history, Instagram and kik messages

    v. See installed apps

    vi. Does not monitor Facebook or Snapchat

5. See what options your phone company, Cable Company providers offer for parental controls and take action.

Let's keep on protecting our children!

While technology offers great benefits from connecting with peers to accessing educational content online, it also creates new challenges for parents. Parents have long faced the dilemma of when to step back and when to take a more hands-on approach with their kids. Technology has added a new wrinkle to that problem. Today's parents must navigate how, when and to what extent they oversee their teens' online and mobile activities. It is our job to protect them in the digital world they live in. Let's keep on protecting our children!

About the Author

Dr. Lauretta Justin is the founder, President and CEO of Millennium Eye Center where she practices optometry. She is an entrepreneur, speaker, author and singer! She is the co-author of the 2011 book "Express Yourself!" In 2015, she released her debut Christmas music album titled, "The Spirit of Christmas!" Both products are available on amazon.

Dr. Lauretta is married to James Justin, her high school sweetheart, and together they have 3 sons. She enjoys reading, singing, playing with her family, and shopping for shoes! To contact her, visit DrLaurettaJustin.com!

Products by the Author

For more information on my latest products, visit amazon.com/author/laurettajustin!

Books:

- Parenting Digital Natives: What parents can do about the danger of social media and online activities of their kids by Dr. Lauretta Justin

- CEO OF YOU: How to Create the Business and the Life of Your Dreams by Dr. Lauretta Justin

- The Power of Prayer by James Justin and Dr. Lauretta Justin

- Christian Counseling by James Justin and Dr. Lauretta Justin

Music CD:

- The Spirit of Christmas by Dr. Lauretta Justin

Parenting Books

1. Positive Parenting: 12 Practical Tips to Prepare your Kids for Success by James Justin

   Tired of yelling and getting nowhere? Imagine... having the tool you need to parent your children! How would you feel to have true family connection! This simple guide shows us how. James offers 12 practical tips to prepare your kids for success.

2. The Dr. James Dobson Parenting Collection by James C. Dobson

   It can be tough to be a mom or dad. Aren't there days when you wish you could sit down with an expert on parenting—somebody who really understands what you're going through and knows just what advice and counsel to give you? Good news: The parenting wisdom you need is here—in one complete volume! In The Dr. James Dobson Parenting Collection, you'll find three bestselling books (The New Dare to Discipline, The New Strong-Willed Child, and Parenting Isn't for Cowards) containing the straightforward, practical, biblical truths you need—from Dr. James Dobson, the world's foremost authority on parenting.

3. 7 Steps to Develop Healthy Relationships with Anyone by James Justin

   Did you know that healthy relationships are an essential link to your success, happiness and well-being? Knowing how to attract, select and nurture healthy relationships within your circle of life will enable you to utilize these relationships as an invaluable source of inspiration, support and strength. These healthy relationships will help you to achieve your goals!

In healthy relationships each member is CELEBRATED rather than TOLERATED.

This book reveals the vital seven steps you must know to attract and maintain healthy relationships with anyone in your personal and business life. If you allow the wrong people in your circle of life, it will have a negative impact on your path to continued success. This book is your key to create the healthy relationships that will unlock your dynamic potential. The steps outlined in this book are life changing. If you read this book and apply its principles, you will not only enjoy BETTER RELATIONSHIPS, you will have a BETTER LIFE!

4. Happiest Baby on the Block by Harvey Karp, M.D.

Dr. Karp, a pediatrician, gives sensible and sweet solutions for new parents to help them handle the screaming fits of their new babies and shares his baby whispering secrets and research. His number one piece of advice to his readers is: "Get help! Throughout history, young couples were never expected to care for a baby all by themselves. Also, enjoy this time—even the challenging moments. Your baby's early months will go by in a blink."

5. How to Talk So Kids Will Listen and Listen So Kids Will Talk by Adele Faber and Elaine Mazlish

You probably already know this: Yelling at and pleading with your children doesn't work. This book offers respectful advice for ways to speak to children. If you want less stress in your family interactions and more love and goodwill, this is for you. It will help you improve relationships--with your kids, yes, but with everyone else you meet, too.

6. The Sleep Easy Solution by Jennifer Waldburger, L.C.S.W., and Jill Spivack, L.C.S.W.

When celebrities with new babies need to get some sleep, they call on these popular Hollywood psychotherapists. Their technique gets babies snoozing in as little as three nights. They aim to address the emotional needs of the parent and the child, including tips and tools for handling the crying of both mom and baby.

7. Brain Rules for Baby by John Medina

Medina, a molecular biologist and a dad, gives advice on how to raise smart and happy children from infancy through age 5. He explains, for instance, why TV watching for kids ages 2 and under is harmful. He also believes the best predictor of performance is not IQ but impulse control. This book, filled with fascinating facts and science, is addictive--be prepared to ignore the kids because it's hard to put down.

8. 1-2-3 Magic: Effective Discipline for Children 2-12 by Thomas W. Phelan. Ph.D.

    In three easy-to-follow steps, Phelan can get your kids to cooperate and bring down your stress level. This indispensable book will help you during mealtimes, meltdowns, homework arguments, and other tricky kid situations. Overall, his tips encourage better behavior from moms and kids. He aims to abolish the "Talk-Persuade-Argue-Yell-Hit" cycle--and his method works. I still use it on my school age children.

9. Positive Discipline by Jane Nelsen, Ed.D.

    This book has been enlightening frustrated parents for more than 25 years. Nelsen, a well-known psychologist, educator, and mother of seven, believes in mutual respect, not punishment. Her techniques are effective, firm, and kind. She teaches parents of toddlers through teenagers to cooperate, communicate, and love each other. Read this book, try out the advice, and watch your household become calmer.

10.   The Baby Book by William Sears, M.D., Martha Sears, R.N., Robert Sears, M.D., and James Sears, M.D.

    Dr. Sears and his family have become trusted authorities on topics including vaccinations, medical interventions, and behavioral issues. This baby bible offers sound advice on eating, sleeping, health, and comfort.

Quotes on Parenting

"Let's keep on protecting our children online and off line! They need it more than ever." Dr. Lauretta Justin

"Children, obey your parents in all things, for this is well pleasing to the Lord. Parents, do not provoke your children to anger by the way you treat them. Rather, bring them up with the discipline and instruction that comes from the Lord." (St. Paul).

"It is easier to build strong children than to repair broken men" (Frederick Douglass).

"Having a baby is a life-changer. It gives you a new perspective on life" (James Justin).

"Always kiss your children goodnight, even if they're already asleep" (H. Jackson Brown, Jr.).

"At the end of the day, the most overwhelming key to a child's success is the positive involvement of parents" (Jane D. Hull).

www.ingramcontent.com/pod-product-compliance
Lightning Source LLC
Chambersburg PA
CBHW031618040426
42452CB00006B/583